FOOD
for thought

The complete book of concepts for growing minds

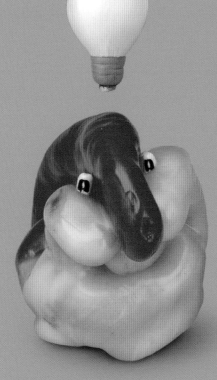

Written and illustrated by Saxton Freymann

ARTHUR A. LEVINE BOOKS

An Imprint of Scholastic Inc. / New York

For Devo and Abi Ihonde

Book design by Elizabeth B. Parisi and Saxton Freymann
Photography by Saxton Freymann and Nimkin/Parrinello

ISBN-13: 978-0-439-11018-1
ISBN-10: 0-439-11018-1

10 9 8 7 6 5 4 3   09 10 11 12 13

Printed in China
First edition, February 2005

FREYMANN, SAXTON

Ingredients: oranges, kumquats, rhubarb, black-eyed peas, assorted broccoli, bell peppers, onions, carrots, portabella, enoki and white-button mushrooms, sesame seeds, mustard seeds, pink and green peppercorns, red grapefruit, kiwifruits, cauliflower, spaghetti squash, starfruit, apples, leek, jumbo scallion, beet juice, strawberries, black beans, lemon, black rice, damson plum, concord grape, Chinese eggplant, sweet potato, black olives, pear stems, artichokes, yellow squash, assorted pears, bananas, cherries, baby pineapples, green Italian peppers, eggplants, brussels sprout, baby corn, bok choy, tomatoes and plum tomatoes, radishes, peaches, endive, assorted cucumbers, beets, celery, blueberries, onion skin, persimmon, pomegranate, mango, broccolini, papayas, snake squash, watermelon, acorn squash, asparagus, zucchini, canary melon, lady apple, nectarine, potatoes, parsley, turnips, fig, okra, daikon radish, jalapeño pepper, honeydew melon, savoy cabbage.

Table of Contents

SHAPES

Circle

Oval

Triangle

Square

Rectangle

Star

Crescent

Diamond

Heart

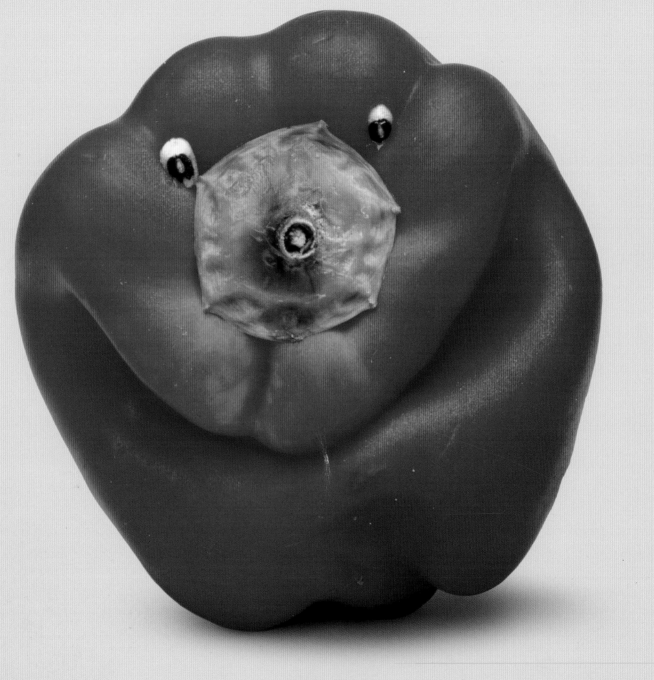

Red

Orange

Yellow

13

Green

Blue

14

Purple

Brown

White
&
Black

COLORS!

1

One bird

2
Two chicks

3
Three giraffes

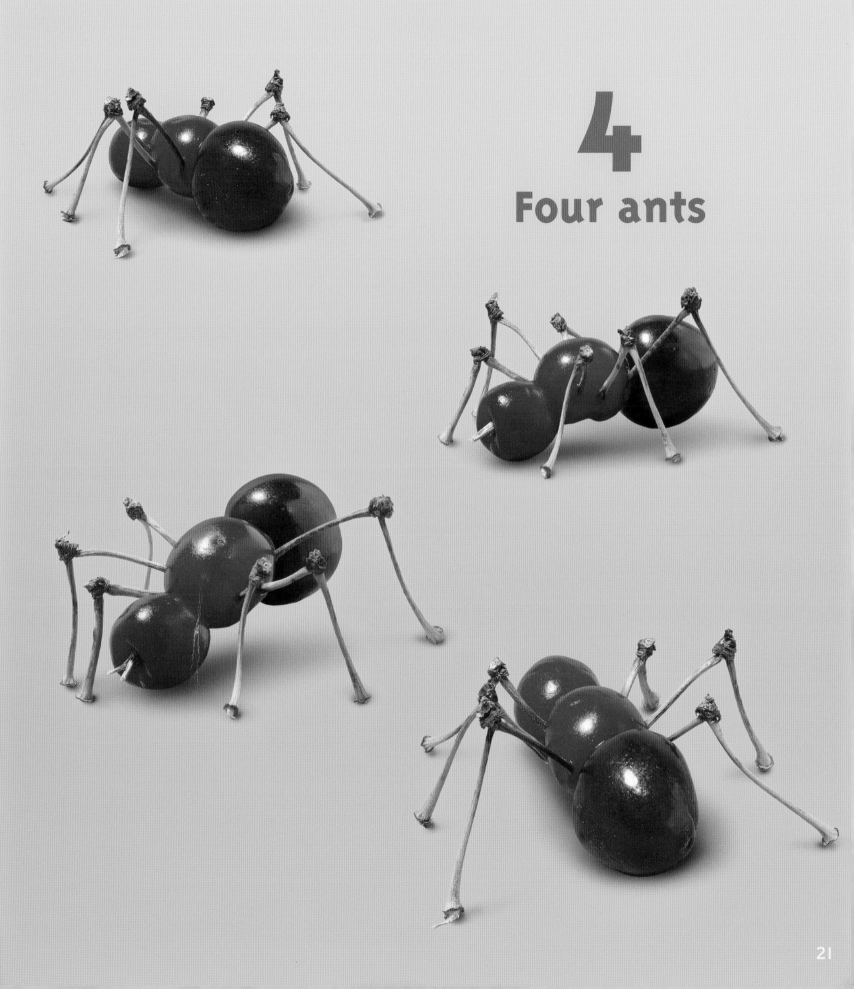

4
Four ants

5
Five turtles

23

24

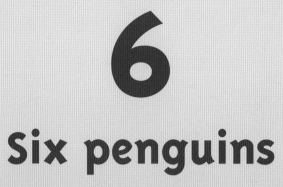

Six penguins

7
Seven fish

8
Eight hippos

30

Nine frogs

10
Ten sheep

A a
Airplane

B b

Bird

C c

Cat

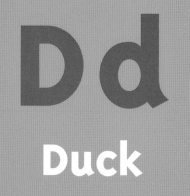

Dd

Duck

Ee

Elephant

Ff
Flower

Gg
Guinea pig

Hh Hair

I i Insects

39

Jj

Jack-in-the-box

Kk
Kangaroo

Ll
Lizard

M m

Monkey

Nn
Nest

Oo
Owl

P p
Pig

Qq

Queen

Rr

Rabbit

S s
Snake

T t
Turtle

Uu

Umbrella

V v
Vegetables

W w
Walrus

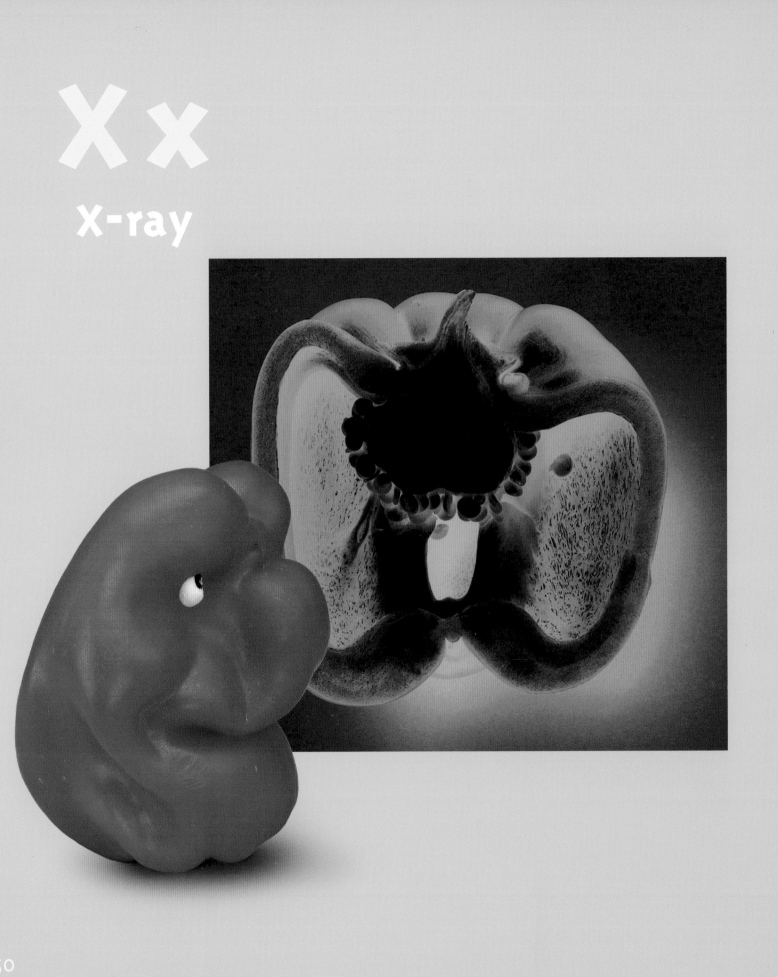

X x

X-ray

Yy
Yo-yo

Zz
Zebra

51

OPPOSITES

Up

Down

Big

Little

53

Happy

Sad

Hot

Cold

Near

Come

Far

Go

Give

Receive

57

Whisper

Shout

Awake

Asleep